Fears that Rhyme

Julie Dunic

BookLeaf
Publishing

India | USA | UK

Presentation by *BookLeaf Publishing*

Web: www.bookleafpub.com

E-mail: info@bookleafpub.com

ISBN: 9789363315297

First edition 2024

*I'm dedicating this book to my younger self.
Hell or high water, we're making a book.*

ACKNOWLEDGEMENT

I would like to thank every writing teacher I've ever had, for guiding me in fine tuning an outlet that has been so precious to me. There is something truly special about writing.

PREFACE

A lot of people (me being one of them) enjoy things that are scary. Scary things are stimulating and bring your mind into a different state than the norm.They elicit a reaction (or at least trigger an association) of fear, which is quite a distinct and intense feeling. By having the ability to expose oneself to scary subject matter- and then get away from it- there's a certain thrill and satisfaction of being in control. Unless the fear sticks, leaving the person lying awake that night in a cold sweat, hyperventilating, questioning every decision they've ever made, which they probably don't enjoy. But hey, they signed up for the risk when they watched that movie or read that book. I think this is a risk everyone should be willing to take.

Werewolf

My wife and I decided to
Go on a little walk,
We often stroll and chat things through,
It's always nice to talk.
We tend to choose a distant trail,
Through forests it would go.
However there was a strong gale,
And rain began to flow.

I turned and danced and spun around
As winds pushed to and fro.
I could no longer stand my ground,
My wife screamed that we go.

Suddenly, just as it came,
The storm had quickly ceased.
It felt as if it played a game,
An indecisive beast.

But then I looked along the path
And through a haggard tree,
It seemed that by the weather's wrath
My wife was lost from me.
I took a step and called her name
Before me and behind,
I looked so hard to find her frame,
Felt I had lost my mind.
The sun had set beyond the hill
Upon that dreary night.
The dark had just begun to spill
Consuming all my sight.
Despite the shadowed land ahead,
The moon still lit the sky,
With glowing clouds, and me, it led,
Straight toward it. How? And Why?

My bones began to throb and ache,
My muscles twitched and burned.
I felt my pupils start to shake,
My stomach flipped and churned.
Now ears and teeth exploded through,
And claws and fur erupted,
My arms and legs got longer, too,

Now thoughts came in corrupted.

I clenched the ground with all four paws,
And looked up towards the moon,
Then opened wide my great big jaws,
I felt like some old loon.
My crazed black eyes went glaring red,
And I inhaled so deep,
Then howled so loud it'd hurt your head,
Might put you right to sleep.

I ran and ran o'er dirt and sticks
My legs and brain were flying,
My beating heart made rapid ticks,
Until I heard some crying.
Possessed by moon my limbs had flown
Right to the flooded lake,
The sound and smell of helpless moan
Just made my senses quake.

The wolf had won, the human gone,
And so was gone, my will.
She looked just like an injured fawn,
Whom I just had to kill.
I tore her flesh to tattered shreds,
Blood dripping down my chest.
Her skin tore just like loose stitched threads,
Her liver tasted best.

I woke up early the next morn,
The tail and teeth had vanished,
I felt as if I'd been reborn,
And certainly not famished.
Well this had not occurred before,
Not ever in my life.
And at my feet was awful gore,
The body of my wife.

Scarecrow

There was a farmer on some land
Where many creatures live.
Hank never had a helping hand
Though he would always give.
The chickens, cows, and sheep galore
Were only just the start,
The donkeys, rabbits, goats and more
With whom he'd never part.

He had one favorite on his plot
That he would always seek,
Hank loved this fellow a whole lot,
Though they could never speak.
The scarecrow's name is Old Plaid Jed,
Who stays out by the crops,
He has big arms, a tiny head,

And stitched on eyes and chops.

For fifty years, the farmer'd check,
To make sure Jed stood right,
And to repair a crow's deep peck
Once it had taken flight.
There was a rule that Jed obeyed
The farmer couldn't know.
That even though from straw he's made,
Jed walks and talks and so…
The farmer would just turn his back
To our friend Jed so frozen,
Then button eyes turned blue from black,
Some threads would come unwoven.
He'd hop down from his stick, carefree
And dance around the field.
You'd think he's looking quite silly,
A shovel he would yield.

However there's a part of him
That felt sad and forlorn,
Alone, depressed, and rather grim
In that big field of corn.
Jed longed for love, maybe a friend,
Just simple company.
A partner staying til the end
In perfect harmony.

"Oh please, just make one more" he'd say,

Though Hank would never hear.
"There's extra clothes and so much hay,
"Please give me my own dear."
There was no hope for silent speech
To men of senior years,
Not even normal sounds would reach
The farmer's faulty ears.

One day Plaid Jed awaited his
Check in with the old man,
He wondered oh what time it is
He normally makes his scan.
The moon came up and sun went down
As hours passed on by.
His smile slowly formed a frown,
While darkness took the sky.

Days came and went with no relief,
Hank simply never showed.
Jed started to exhibit grief
And his straw heart felt low.
He then realized he was alone,
With no-one near to see,
So he jumped down, let out a groan,
And walked forth dangerously.

Jed quickly came upon the farm,
Where Hank was surely hiding,
He couldn't see what was the harm

Of a brief scarecrow sighting.
Jed searched around and found the door,
And then to his dismay,
Saw Hank collapsed down on the floor,
His flesh green with decay.

Then Jed began to hatch a plan
To answer both his cries.
He dragged Hank's body out and ran
To hay bales stacked up high.
Jed stuffed Hank up with fists of straw
Piled straight into his mouth,
He nearly broke off Hank's old jaw
As fistfuls traveled south.

Green goo and blood escaped his skin
As Jed would not stop going.
Until the straw would not fit in
He really started slowing.
Then finally Jed looked around,
Deciding he was finished.
Not any soul there made a sound,
The hay bales were diminished.

But in an instant Hank convulsed,
And Jed fell to the floor,
He was at least a bit repulsed
At how Hank was restored.

.

"Hello" Hank coughed through straw and air
And looked at his old bud.
Jed gawked at him with a blank stare
With all the mess and blood.

The two will stand in crops so still,
And guard it all from crows.
But sometimes they just need a fill,
And dance from heads to toes.
Hank still loves all his cows and goats
And all the other's with them,
He still goes 'round and feeds them oats,
And now Jed just goes with him.

Ouija

The three girls stared down at the board,
It had to be restored.

There were some stains and corners torn
With golden letters worn.

They took it home to wait for dark,
Then brought it to the park.

They sat around what they had found,
Right on the dirty ground.

Upon the planchette, hands were placed,
And true dark fears were faced.

They asked if any ghosts were there

And had some things to share.

Next one girl had a funny thought,
And she began to plot.

She moved their hands and spelled things out.
The other two showed doubt.

As moon rose higher in the sky,
She still went on to lie.

Their hands kept moving through the night,
Which started causing fright.

"Who's doing this?' The first girl said,
And looked up with her head.

"Not me!" The shaking second cried.
"Or me," The liar sighed.

They asked the board some questions more,
The two girls weren't sure.

The first girl asked "What's going on?
"Hey Ghost, can you be gone?"

"I did it!" third girl then exclaimed,
"There's no ghost to be blamed!"

The two girls didn't say a word,
Directed at the third.

"I'm scared and cold let's go right now!"
The first girl raised her brow.

"I hate this too!" the second moaned,
"Let's leave the board," she groaned.

"Come on you two, it's just been me!"
The third then laughed with glee.

She picked the planchette up and beamed
But then the others screamed.

She laughed amused by her own gloating,
To them, the planchette was just floating.

They had not heard a word she said,
It's then she realized, she was dead.

Bugs

Everything in Elle's life
Was just always very clean,
If ever there was any dirt,
She'd always cause a scene.
She hired maids and cleaners that
Exclusively lived-in,
But what she cared for most of all
Was her dear, precious skin.
She had skin care collections,
Cleansers, face masks by the tub,
And her top favorite thing was
To go get a body scrub.
She walked into the spa one day
And got a room for one,

And told them just exactly what
It was she wanted done.
The music sounded quiet and
Relaxing with dim light,
It smelled like incense in the room
And she felt less uptight.
Eyes closed she laid buck naked on
The table clean and warm,
Elle loved the sense of being fresh
And getting to transform.
Facedown she heard soft foot steps gently
Enter in the room,
She'd feel scrub in an instant she would
Naturally assume.
Instead of damp and warm and nice
Upon her spotless back,
She felt a new sensation that
Just made her want to yack.
These things spilled down on her lovely skin
That creeped and crept and crawled,
She couldn't move, she was so scared,
And then she simply bawled.
Some seconds passed, it didn't stop,
The creatures piled up,
The more there were, the more they moved,
It seemed they riled up.
Her eyes then opened wide and she
Let out horrific screams,
For what was on the floor was even

Worse than her worst dreams.
Spiders, ants, and crickets too were
Wriggling down below her,
Beetles, worms, and cockroaches
But they were a bit slower.
She felt their legs and specks of dirt
Right on her sterile flesh,
She'd have to burn off all her skin
From this to be clean, fresh.
Miss Elle kept staying frozen as she
Was so paralyzed,
The more and more time passed, the more
The bugs went up in size.
Some flies and moths and bees appeared to
Add into the group,
She felt their toes and tongues and even
Surely some small poop.
Elle gagged; her sugar, floral scent now
Truly badly tainted,
At this point she felt so, so bad
That she knocked out and fainted.
They went into her ears and nose and
Even in her mouth,
Some made their way down to the holes
That were all way down south.
Staff found her the next morning; their top
Client most invested;
There wasn't even skin left because
It was so infested.

Jack-O-Lantern

A pumpkin
is a pumpkin
until it has a face.
Then,
a Jack-O-Lantern
is born.

On a late, October evening,
a man
gutted
and carved the flesh
of his prized gourd.
Its mouth hole angry,
its eye holes mischievous…

The next morning,
it was
missing.

Little did he know,
the Jack-O-Lantern was
hob-hob-hobbling
down the road.
A little girl saw it
while riding her bike
and crashed.

The Jack-O-Lantern
stopped
at a small building.
It twisted its vines
up above itself,
and opened the door
of the local morgue.

The Jack-O-Lantern
slithered around,
furling and unfurling
its foliage
onto the bodies—
only the headless ones.

A fat one? A thin one? A man? A child? One
with a lot of body hair?

One with a good build?
Aha.

The Jack-O-Lantern
wriggled its appendages
into the neck,
and walked away.

The Jack-O-Lantern
became a successful
plumber,
and married a beautiful woman.
She loved
his unique orange face
(only his face was orange)
and his simple features.

The Jack-O-Lantern
had a daughter one day.
She had
her mother's face,
and her father's body.
It was hard
to find clothes
that fit her,
and she always smelled like pumpkin pie.

Zombies

Close your blinds, lock your door.
Be on guard, don't ignore,
Any sight, any smell.
When they come, you just yell.
They come creep, night or day.
They won't ever, stay away.

You hear them early, right at dawn,
Making their way up your lawn.
Scratchy clinks, of their bones,
Hollow clanks, ghastly groans.
They don't breath, there's just air,
Traveling through their mouths and hair;
Deep whistling through their empty caverns,

Like wind through an abandoned tavern.

You hear them banging on your wall,
They'll stop at really nothing at all.
Although they're dead, they still hunger,
Tearing up the town asunder.
They've killed and killed, ate all they could,
They're spreading through the neighborhood.
If you live it takes just one bite,
Remember that when you go fight.

Your door starts cracking with their weight,
You brace yourself to meet your fate.
They have dark bags under their eyes,
Grey cheeks, blue lips, dehumanized.
Their forms are gaunt, their limbs all bent,
It's clear that all their lives are spent.
Some body parts have come detached
Some of them have parts mismatched.

They break in; burst into the room,
Dozens and dozens with a BOOM!
The mailman missing half his jaw,
Crawling over, dead skin raw.
Ms. Calvins from the doctor's billing,
With open wounds and guts out-spilling.
Your teacher from the second grade,
Could surely use some good first aid.

But no more zombie spreading here,
You shoot them up from ear to ear.
You put an end to all their gains,
And put a bullet in their brains.
Your walls vibrate from every shot,
All of them can die and rot!
BANGBANGBANG, four, five, fifty more,
Now all their bodies are on the floor.

Congrats, whoopee, you go eat some chips.
There's not much else to do during an
apocalypse.

Vampire

Every Thursday night I had
My dreaded shift at 2 am.
I'd always drive down oh, so mad,
I'd really always felt condemned.

But something happened there last week
That truly made me horrified,
I'm typically always quite weak,
But still I swear I almost died.

I pulled up at the booth at 2
My eyes already very heavy.
Barely any cars drove through,

With bills or coins for me to levy.

I sat in the small, windowed room,
I stared down at my dirty shoes.
Outside was black and dark and doom,
This job I really didn't choose.

Then something in the night came by,
Against the window in the door.
It really caught me by surprise,
That ended all my painful bore.

A bat hung there, full upside down,
Right at the top, wings tightly wrapped,
With pointed ears, just like a crown.
Right then I felt like I'd been trapped.

It looked at me with its black eyes,
And then it started to transform.
It seemed the bat was just a guise,
First came a human leg, then arm.

It grew in size and turned real pale,
And almost all its hair fell off.
It looked quite dainty, but not frail;
Her face was strong, yet it was soft.

She still hung upside down right there,
Her eyes still cold and heartless black,

And somehow I just had to stare,
Her beauty taken me aback.

Her tiny fingers traced the glass,
And I felt them caress my face.
Right then I started feeling crass,
She had such poise and haunting grace.

I saw her start to hover left,
And slowly, she encircled me.
My mind had fully gone bereft,
She smiled but it wasn't glee.

Her long black hair was down so low,
Her skin was stark against the night.
She gazed right at me, down below,
Red lips with fangs so gleaming white.

She wanted me to let her in,
And I was tempted to obey.
"Unlock the door" her mind summoned;
I knew I had to stay away.

Beyond her hypnotizing thought,
I tried so hard to block her out.
It knew it was my blood she sought,
I knew she could not go without.

Then she rotated to the floor,

Like softly falling fragile fabric.
She faced me; I could not ignore,
Her essence, alluringly tragic.

The ebony eyes penetrated mine,
I watched my hand reach for the lock.
She nodded as to say "all's fine,"
And smiled, fixed her hair, and frock.

My body was beyond control,
It opened the up the door with ease.
I felt as if she had my soul,
For her, I'd sink down to my knees.

And then my mouth spoke words for me,
It was that moment that she'd win.
Just two words would let her be free,
I spoke the words she'd need: "Come in."

She entered through the door inside,
And I went limp into her arms.
Her smile went a little snide,
But of mystique and tempting charms.

I had succumbed to her sweet scent,
Could not resist her energy,
Her presence, I could not repent,
Her spirit gave me lethargy.

She leaned down slow straight toward my neck,
I desperately yearned for her bite.
I didn't care of the effect,
Her teeth were dripping with moonlight.

She bit right down and drunk me dry,
My brain was beyond ecstatic.
Within her grip, I thrashed and writhed,
Euphoria; it was fantastic.

I closed my eyes and felt so warm,
I opened them, they changed to black.
Blissful, elated, I was to reform,
And to that job, I won't go back.

Doll

The mom was full of sad chagrin,
Since Grandma was so tardy.
It badly hurt because it was Corinne's
Sixth birthday party.

She came in fake designer clothes,
And said hello to no-one.
A smile never fit her pose,
So she would never show one.

Corinne unwrapped the doll from her;
Antique, petite, and frail.
She hadn't put much effort in,
It came from some yard sale.

The doll then sat upon a shelf,

Above the girl's small bed.
Corinne then wondered to herself
The things she left unsaid:

How could she play in any way
Without the doll just breaking?
There must be something that's okay
They both could be partaking.

Corinne stared at its porcelain frame,
And pretty purple dress.
If only they could play a game,
And cause a little stress.

She grabbed the doll right by the hair;
And started chopping locks.
Brown ringlets fell, without a care,
She'd keep them in a box.

Corinne grabbed paints and markers, too
And started scribbling lines.
The pink lips gone, and cheeks now blue,
And colors of all kinds.

But still, the doll's green eyes shown through,
So deep and clear and real.
It truly seemed like they had view,
And they could really feel.

Of course, Corinne got bored again,
What could she do instead?
She jabbed the doll's neck with a pen,
And then pried off its head.

Her mother came into the room
And started acting brash.
She would not let Corinne resume,
And threw it in the trash.

One day, Corrine came home from school,
With bunches of hair shaved.
Some gum had gotten stuck, how cruel.
Her hair could not be saved.

Next morning she woke up and flinched
When she saw her reflection,
She had a rash on every inch,
It was some weird infection.

She tried some creams and capsules too,
But nothing worked at all.
Her skin was green, red, yellow, blue;
She looked just like her doll.

And then it happened late that night,
They really were the same.
It was such an unpleasant sight,
But no-one was to blame.

Corinne caught butterflies outside,
She was so fascinated.
A branch snapped on her neck; she died.
She was decapitated.

Before her mother came to see,
And feel the utter horror,
She went to find some jewelry
And opened up her drawer.

As soon as she looked down in there,
She felt such awful dread.
'Cause looking back was the cold stare
Of the small porcelain head.

Skeleton

I was strollin all around in the town graveyard
One midnight in the Fall.
The sky was black and very starred,
From what I can recall.
There were old graves, some tall some short.
They were all shapes and sizes.
And then I swear I can report
That graveyard had surprises.

Beneath the shroud of moonlit dark
Some skeletons appeared.
I know it seems a false remark,
I know that it sounds weird.
They clawed their way out of the Earth,
With boney hands at ease.
It's like they had all been rebirthed,

And did just as they pleased.

They shook off all the dirt and roots
From skull to their phalanges.
Then they all signed a quick salute,
And ran around so dandy.
I stared while they cavorted 'round
The age old cemetery.
They danced and hopped and made some
bounds,
It looked so grand and merry.

They passed their skulls down like batons
It looked like jaws were cackling.
It was a whole routine, full on,
The older bones were crackling.
The sounds they made while skipping
Were an empty hollow knocking,
Each step they were so close to slipping,
The whole thing was so shocking.

The bats went screech and crows went caw,
And wind howled through the trees.
The whole event had me in awe,
It was a symphony.
And so they danced among tomb stones
Their pace, increasing speed.
They kept on juggling more, more bones,
As if it was their creed.

Ribs went by with fibula,
With tarsals, femurs, too.
Scapulas and tibia,
The list of loose bones grew.
At last they lay their deconstructed,
Pieces strewn about.
Their dance had been very corrupted
If this was the fall out.

The sounds had stopped and things were still
So I walked to the scene.
As I approached I got a chill,
Bones nowhere to be seen.
The sun was out so I looked hard,
Like I was in a trance.
But nothing was in the graveyard
Of the creepy skeleton dance.

Skinwalker

We were camping in the woods by the lake
And although it was late,
My friends wanted to stay awake.
One said "Let's play manhunt,
"It'll be a great stunt."
"In the dark, in the trees,"
Everyone agrees.

So we ran and I hid behind a log
Near the bog,
And through the fog
I saw a dog.
But the dog wasn't right,
Even in black night,
I could see its mouth tight,

Its tall height,
And the legs bent out just slight.
It came toward me in silhouette.
And I began to sweat
Because it seemed a threat.

I noticed my friend looking around,
He'd already found
Some in hiding.
It looked like they were dividing
To find where I was residing.
The creature lurched forward
And came quickly toward
My frozen self.
No-one else
Could see the glowing eyes,
The shoulders rise,
And the unnatural cries
As the thing stood up high.

I felt my shoulder grasped
And then I gasped
As I turned to my friend grinning.
He told me he was close to winning.
I looked back and gone was my stalker.
Everyone thought I was just a talker.
No-one believed I'd seen a skinwalker.

Ghost

They'd heard there were spirits
In the remains of the old house
Deep in the woods.

They approached at dusk,
Using only their flashlights,
To guide them
Over vines and rocks,
And fallen branches,
And the uneven earth
Beneath their feet.
It was but
Only an infinitesimal
Circle of visibility,

In the never-ending,
Omnipotent
Air of dark.

But eventually
They found
The measly piles of bricks,
And stone pillars,
That once made up the house;
A skeleton
Of what once stood.
There were fragments
Of walls and stairs,
Creating a juvenile labyrinth
Of sorts.
But in the black mask of night,
Amongst the shadows,
There were many places
For something to be out of sight.

The structure seemed alive itself;
So intricate, so lived in.
Although the bulk of the house was gone,
It was clear,
Every piece that stood the test of time,
Was part of something bigger.

The tiny moon was only a sliver in the sky,
Teasing them

With its illumination,
Barely coming through.

As they walked and looked,
They saw how the vines and plants
Seeped through the bricks;
Outgrew them.
They were vandalized by graffiti,
And initials carved in the stone.

Beyond that,
There were just trees,
Looming over them,
Smothering them,
Breathing over them in the wind.
Layers upon layers of
Branches and intricate shadows,
Getting deeper and blacker.

A chill rushed through the air
On a cold breeze,
Cutting through their bones,
Pressing them to shiver suddenly.

In that moment,
In the blink of an eye,
They saw her.

Through the delicate luminescence

Of the moon,
A glowing white form appeared.
She hovered, more fragile than glass,
And fainter than a cloud on a foggy day,
Almost completely untraceable to most senses.
But they felt her.
She stood,
Barely a whisper
In a forest of screams.

Her face was featureless;
An elegant, airy shape,
Gazing to the side
With a hand to her chin.
Although there were no eyes or mouth,
There was still a mystical, ethereal
Beauty about her.

She radiated the softest glow,
Bringing to life only the gentlest
Touch of grays and greens and browns
To the stones and grass around her
In the dark.

Her lower half was obscured
Behind the remains of a wall.
But the few stars in the sky
Reflected into her angelic, flowing gown
Before them.

And then, she was gone.
Although they could no longer see her,
The overwhelming presence of someone else
Stayed.
The air was heavy,
But in a way that compelled them
To stay.
Their bodies weighed them down,
As if she wanted them
To stay.
She wanted her home to be remembered.

Clown

When I was a child,
The Circus came to town.
It all seemed so wild,
Tigers, acrobats, and clowns.

With popcorn in hand,
I popped in my seat.
The place was so crammed,
I could just fit my feet.

The ringmaster came,
We saw magic and more.
I thought most of it lame,
Just one act wasn't a bore.

A tiny car appeared,

Out came clown after clown.
I found it really weird,
And a bit profound.

They made jokes and did tricks,
Each squirted a squirt gun.
They did splits, cartwheels, kicks....
It was odd but so fun.

They had caked on white face paint,
And weird painted eyes,
Costumes massive but quaint
And big shoes the wrong size.

Right after the show I snuck out
To the trucks.
The clowns all had stuck out,
Their moves always in flux.

I found them nearby,
Right behind the big tent.
And now this begins why,
I was filled with regret.

With faces washed off,
And white faces revealed.
I was so caught off
Guard 'cause their white skin was real.

Their noses stayed giant
With makeup removed.
I stayed oh, so silent,
Completely unmoved.

Their eyes were all beady,
Without fun colored shapes.
And they moved fast and speedy,
Like they wanted escape.

They peeled off their shoes
And their gloves of white suede.
I was so confused,
And at this point afraid.

Beneath all of that
Unfurled giant sharp claws.
I got the urge to leave, stat,
But I just had to pause.

With big noses in the air,
They sniffed hard all around.
Then they jumped, I swear,
In a hole in the ground.

I waited a second,
Came out to patrol.
The mystery beckoned,
So I looked down the hole.

It was so tremendous,
It was like some weird dream.
It was black and seemed endless.
Then I heard a child's scream.

I rushed back to my friends,
The scream haunting my soul.
But they couldn't comprehend,
Clowns are just giant moles.

Halloween

Randal hated Halloween,
He loathed it every year.
He lived by lots of snot-nosed kids,
They'd come from far and near.
They'd all come flocking to his door
With trick or treat bags out,
They'd smell and scream and pester him,
"Go scram!" he'd always shout.

This year he had a great idea
To rid them from his lawn.
He'd poison up some tasty treats,
So they'd be dead by dawn.
He gathered up some chocolate bites,

And toxins he injected.
And soon enough, he couldn't wait,
They all would be ingested.

The Fall wind blew and children walked,
And leaves fell in the air.
Pumpkins sat on every step,
And black cats sat and stared.
An hour passed or maybe more,
And then the first knock came
Upon his door, and Randal ran,
It was just like a game.

A devil, witch and ghost stood there,
They wore full suits and masks.
He grinned with glee at his first prey,
And he fulfilled his task.
They thanked him and continued.
Randal stood there so perplexed,
Was glad, intoxicated,
Couldn't wait to see who's next.

Zombies, werewolves, cowboys, more
Came by with no good warning.
Mummies, cats and fairies
Wouldn't make it til next morning.
The moon came up and time went by,
The kids seemed to be done.
Randal called it for the night,

He'd had a lot of fun.

But then, again, his doorbell rang,
He shrugged and checked the door.
It was the devil, witch and ghost
Who'd been there way before.
"You're back?" he said and opened up
They all said "Trick or treat!"
He didn't mind them having more
Of poisoned goods to eat.

He said good night and settled down
And tucked himself in bed.
But that same knocking came once more,
So he covered up his head.
It wouldn't stop so he got up,
Ran to the door and then,
Got mad, for on his porch
Stood those three same odd kids again.

He screamed at them and slammed the door
And turned out all his lights.
He almost fell asleep
But then he got a real true fright.
The knocking started in his ears,
This time it sounded close.
This was because this time
It came from his bedroom windows.

He stomped towards them and spat right through
The old school window screen.
They scurried off, he didn't care if
That was maybe too mean.
Randal sighed and shut his eyes
And quickly fell to sleep.
But then in the full dead of night
He awakened from a peep.

They all lay there right next to him,
They smelled so sugary sweet.
They whispered three soft words to him
And told him "Trick or treat!"
He jolted up, and pushed them off,
Turned on his bedside lamp.
His night clothes stuck tight to his skin,
They were so sweaty damp.

"Get out!" he roared and grabbed the witch
And pulled her mask straight off.
But then he screamed, for underneath
The mask made him go soft.
It seemed they ate those candies long
Before he had discovered.
It seemed they were all dead because
Their clothes were empty and hovered.

Boogeyman

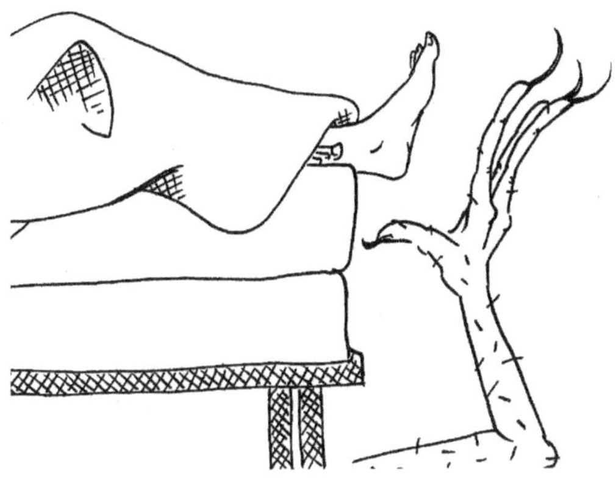

My parents tuck me into bed
And Mommy pats my little head.
Daddy says there's nothing to fear,
But they haven't seen the monsters here.

Mom says I have bad dreams, is all,
But she doesn't know how they slink, how they
crawl!
My parents' words just make me sigh:
"You're dreaming! You're playing a game!
Don't lie!"

Mommy and Daddy give kisses good night,
And walk out of the room and turn off the light.
What happens then makes me almost vomit,
As I see them slowly emerge from my closet.

More creep out from under my bed loudly
screaming,
They're laughing, it's evil, I wish I were
dreaming!
They claw at my hair,
Their stench fills the air!

Goosebumps rise upon my skin,
Sheer terror erupts from deep within.
Their giant, sharp teeth drooling horrid and
jagged,
Their fur is knotted and terribly ragged.

At last, I summon the courage to run,
I'm tired of giving them so much fun!
As I jump off the bed, they reach for my arm,
A claw slits my hand, but it wasn't much harm.

I book it out fast and hear the door slam,
They shriek and they wail but I just yell
"scram!"
Will they truly never, ever leave me?
Will Mommy and Daddy ever believe me?

I dash to their room and hug them and cry.
They roll their eyes and ask me why.
I tell them how the creatures hide,
I swore it, trying to confide.

"You're fine," they say, "Go back to sleep."
All I could do was plead, and weep.

But soon enough, I slept between them,
Yet when I wake up, I do not see them.
I'm in my room, all tucked in bed,
It really messes with my head.

The monsters don't exist, I deem.
The whole event was a bad dream.

But what I don't hear Mommy say
Is "I can't take these dreams one more day!"
And what I don't hear Dad reply
Is "He's getting heavy, I can't deny

"I struggled to carry him back to his bed.
"He'll be confused too, it'll mess with his head."
I wipe my tears and feel some pain,
Then see my hand is cut, blood stained.

I gasp and stop breathing from what I had found,
And hear that familiar snarling around.

Alien

The man fell fast asleep
As soon as he turned off the light.
But unbeknownst to him
This would begin a crazy night.
A saucer spun above
His roof enormous and so bright,
But it had a protective
Field to block it off from sight.
The center opened up
And it let out an intense white.

The rays went down into
The man and got him up for flight.
The window opened up
And though he got through, it was tight.

He stayed asleep and snored
All while he went through this odd plight.
He floated up into
The disc just like a measly kite.
Green men were waiting there
Inside, so filled with much excite.

They had big heads with little
Legs and an even smaller bite.
They had the man face down
So he'd have to get up to fight,
And also they could see
His neck which was the transplant site.
Then cut a hole below
His nape, but it was only slight.
Inside they put a chip
And healed it up, it was their rite.

The man woke up and they
Interrogated him, but so polite.
Their eyes were black and he
Felt very tall amongst their height.
They showed him 'round the ship
And how the whole thing was alight.
The green men had devices
Far ahead of human's might,
Machines and switches so
Complex for him to well recite.

They told him mysteries
He'd never know without insight.
To them the secrets of
The universe were only trite.
They knew all future and
The past but tried to just highlight.
The man was fascinated
But his mind was still affright.
He asked if they'd be sending
Him back home at all tonight.

They laughed and said they weren't
Keeping him, it was alright.
They slowly floated him
Back down to bed just like a spright.
He was asleep but he
Woke up and jolted straight upright.
He had the most peculiar
Dream that he wished he could write,
He tried but still no matter
What his memory couldn't cite.

The dream had vanished from
His brain but he still felt uptight,
There was a pain deep in
His neck, of which he felt contrite.

Possession

The priest walked up the stairs
His crucifix and Bible close.
Already deep in prayer,
He knew the house would be morose.

His bag held holy water,
Candles, oils, blessed crosses.
Anything to help the daughter
And prevent potential losses.

The maid showed him the room
That held the girl tied up so tight.
He instantly felt gloom
And set up to perform the rite.

She lay in satin sheets

Under a grandiose canopy.
She eyed him like a treat
With hints of sure insanity.

He laid out all his tools
On an expensive, ornate dresser,
The girl called them all fools,
And that he was not her oppressor.

The mother then cried
And brother winced,
The father shook his head.
The daughter looked snide,
She seemed convinced,
That there would be bloodshed.

Her hair was loose and knotty,
And her eyes were sickly grey.
Scratches covered her whole body,
Teeth had started to decay.

The priest held up his vial
Of the holy water high,
He said things from the Bible.
She responded they would die.

He splashed her and she smirked,
But that did not deter him yet.
He'd just begun his work

And didn't see her as a threat.

The sheet rose up to cover her
Completely on its own.
The mom went to recover her,
But then she made a groan.

The priest waved his large cross around,
The girl then hesitated.
The word of God, he'd then resound,
But then she levitated.

The family gasped,
And furniture crashed
Violently to the floor.
She spoke with a rasp,
Her ropes, she grasped,
And pulled, and then they tore.

The priest splashed oils and got louder,
The demon had to leave.
She sneered and bragged about her power,
And called them all naive.

She still lay floating in the air,
And then to their sheer terror,
Blood spirted out from everywhere,
It seemed to last forever.

They wiped off all their faces
And the room then really wreaked.
It had gotten in all places,
Then the mother really shrieked.

The girl went to the ceiling,
Started crawling weirdly fast,
The brother started reeling,
And the father was aghast.
"The power of Christ compels you!"
The priest said from his chest.
The sheet fell and the small girl threw
A face only satan could express.

The lights and candles all went out
And then the room was dark.
The priest announced they were devout,
And lit a match for spark.

He held it up but they could only hear
The girl's quick crawling.
He swung the crucifix, severe,
The mother was straight bawling.

Then suddenly the girl appeared
So close, before the flame.
The priest repressed his immense fear,
And demanded it give up its claim.

She snarled, spit and cursed
And said these truly heinous things.
Some sentences complete perverse,
The priest said "God is King!"

The girl then fell upon the ground,
The room felt so much lighter.
The family gathered all around
And said she was a fighter.
"My baby girl" the mother stroked
Her daughter's face, now coarse.
The demon now had been revoked.
The girl woke, said "Where's my horse?
"What's with the blood? Why does it stink?
"Where's my new skirt?" she expressed,
"You know," Mom couldn't help but think,
"I liked you better possessed."

Shark

I loved to scuba dive and see
The waters down below.
It was for sure my very favorite
Place by far to go.
The creatures beckoned me with their such
Vastly different life.
It was truly a refuge when
I found myself in strife.
The fish would dance and plants would bloom
And even rocks would swim,
I treasured every minute 'til
That day when things turned grim.
I'd swum all day and saw great sights with
Sunlight shining blue,
But then I saw a great white shark and

Immediately withdrew.
It had scarred fins and angry eyes with
Massive sharp white teeth.
I'd noticed rocks with barnacles and
Swiftly hid beneath.
It was too late, it saw me move and
Its eyes quickly doubled,
It was right in that moment when
I knew I was in trouble.
I swam and kicked my flippers with
As much force as I could,
But I knew compared to it my swimming
Wasn't very good.
It shot right after me with its
Gills heaving, tail nonstop,
I moved so fast it felt as if
My lungs were going to pop.
An orange school of fish came through
I hoped would be distraction,
The shark kept going, didn't even
Have any reaction.
I grabbed some seaweed, threw it back
To maybe block my path,
But it was ineffective to the
Shark or its great wrath.
Now because I scuba dived
I feel like I'm a dummy,
Because these days I just hang out
Inside the shark's big tummy.

Mummy

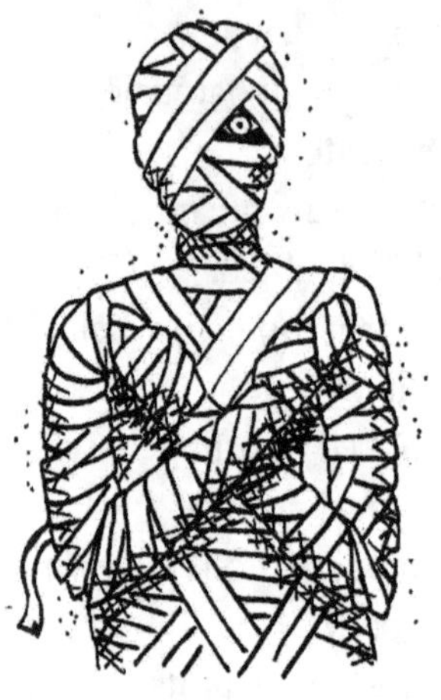

They traveled far and wide to look
Inside the ancient pyramid.
There was just one thing that they took,
All else was far off of the grid.

They found him all wrapped up in gauze,
Inside a great sarcophagus.
They took him quick without a pause,
'Cause traveling was such a fuss.

His dead old smell was so unique,
With bandages so yellowed.
The looked at him with all techniques,
And filmed and scanned the fellow.

One thing that hid somewhere unknown
Were the canopic jars,
Inside of which organs were thrown.
They couldn't have been far.

When people died back in the day,
Their insides were removed.
It helped slow down how they'd decay,
And afterlife improved.

Viscera must stay with the dead,
It's what Egyptians said.
It helped rid afterlife of dread,
It's what all the scrolls read.

The pyramid was such a maze,
That jars could not be found.
They had been looking days and days,
Got turned and turned around.

So then the mummy laid upon
The big X-ray machine.
All these tests took very long,
To see what could be seen.

His skeleton beheld them on the
Great big giant screen.
They gasped and smiled looking at the
Ancient man, unseen.

They went to bed that night excited
At what that day had brought.
One man stayed late, he was delighted,
At what the scans had taught.

Early in the morning they
Got back into the lab.
It seemed the last guy had to pay;
They found him on the slab.
The dead man stood above his chest
With bloody tools and parts.
A mummy on a morbid quest
To dig out a new heart.

Kaiju

Giant wings
Crashed through the sky,
As the creature steered away
Away from the bullets.
The rush of air
Sent ungodly tornados
Whirling around the city,
Demolishing everything in their paths.
BANG BANG BANG!
The soldiers stood their ground.

The monster was just
A gargantuan
Blur of yellow.
It let out an ear shattering
"QUAAAAAAAACK!"
With its beak,
And touched down.

Orange webbed feet
Crushing cars and small buildings.

Mothers clutched their babies.
Families ran into their basements.
The tanks were coming in.
Planes made dizzying circles around it,
Shooting as many bullets and bombs as they
could.

It brought its head low to the ground
But its tail swung up,
Obliterating a bunch of sky scrapers.
People jumped out of windows,
Climbed down fire escapes.
Children let out blood curdling screams.

"QUAAAAACK!"
It wailed again,
Breaking all the glass in the city.
It tried to block
With its wings.
But giant golden feathers
Kept spilling,
Gracefully hovering down,
Suffocating anyone they landed on.

"Please God no!"
"What do we do?!"

"What's happening?!"
Sounded through the streets.
The monster waddled down the highway,
The Earth vibrating with every step.

It launched planes left and right with its wings.
Fires blazed up the night sky
As firefighters tried powerlessly
To diminish the flames.

Suddenly,
A large truck arrived on the scene.
"ATTENTION CITIZENS ATTENTION
CITIZENS!"
It blared through all the sirens.
"WE HAVE BREAD!"
They urgently declared
Through a megaphone.
A message of hope,
Of victory.
An announcement of salvation.

The back of the truck opened.
Men stood lined up,
Throwing baguette after baguette
Into the streets of despair,
As the truck lead the creature towards the ocean.
"QUACKQUACKQUACKQUACKQUACK!"
It bellowed excitedly.

But then it wobbled.
Its eyes went crossed.
Its massive frame came plummeting down.
For the bread had been poisoned.

The city then began picking up the pieces
Of civilization.
As the limp body
Was carried to the water by helicopter,
It let out one final
"Quaaaaaaack."
And then was swallowed up by the sea.

Witch

Beware the old witch that lives
Deep in the marsh,
Her methods of magic
Are really quite harsh.
She's green as pond scum
With hair orange as fire,
Although she seems jolly,
She's really a liar.
She's fat and has boils
And always wears black,
And sometimes she munches
On worms as a snack.
Her nose looks just like
A big carrot, so pointed,

Her cottage is messy
And very disjointed.
There's spell book and potion and
Crystal collections,
And of course a black cat with
The utmost affection.
She'll ask what you want
With her eyes twinkling red,
Then she'll sprinkle some potions
Right onto your head.
She'll smile and nod like
She did you a favor,
But something seems off about
This potion's flavor.
She'll pinch your cheek hard and
Giggle so sweet,
But I swear you're not in
For a very good treat.
"I can grant any wish"
She'll dramatically goad,
But really she just turned you
Into a toad.

Slasher

Five teenagers stay a weekend at a cabin in the woods over Spring Break in the 80s. This is their story…

They were so glad there were five.
The more ideas they could contrive,
More games, activities could thrive.
But they were tired from the drive.
It was late when they had reached the hive,
And from lots of rain, a flood derived,
And so, they slept when they arrived.
But someone broke through the window with a jive.
They were dressed in rags like they were deprived,
And a skeleton mask, like they had connived.
They stabbed one girl, she didn't survive.

Now sadly there were only four.
They found her body full of gore,
And were immediately deplored.
But the killer wasn't there anymore.
They split in groups of two to explore,
And searched each closet, and every door.
One wanted to check the basement floor,
But his partner felt queasy to the core.
"It's fine, I'll go alone," he swore.
So he went downstairs. It was fine, he was sure.
Then the killer bashed him with a drawer.

Then they were reduced to three,
But again, the figure, they didn't see.
They decided it was time to flee,
And began to look for the car key.
In cabinets, on tables, they searched thoroughly.
The lights went out, they cried "Why me?!"
One went outside for the lantern swiftly.
Someone sliced her right inside the knee
And shoved her straight into a tree.

This had brought them down to two,
They'd have to stay close, to make it through.
The key was found, and so they flew.
They started the car, but it barely moved—
From all the mud, and rain only grew.
The guy got out and pushed to make do.

The girl rammed the gas with her shoe.
As soon as it budged, as if on cue,
A knife came through his chest, then turned
askew.

Finally there was only one,
And she was absolutely done.
She recalled the glovebox held a gun.
So she grabbed it, ready for fun.
The killer saw, but didn't run.
She shot it once and her eardrums spun.
The windshield broke but she hadn't won.
The killer punched the glass with the force of a
ton,
And slit her throat, they were down to none.